## Also by Jon Macks

*Heaven Talks Back*

*From Soup to Nuts: The Cannibal Lover's Cookbook*

# fuhgeddaboutit

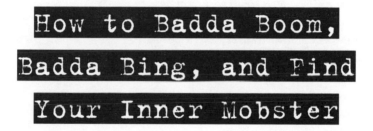

## How to Badda Boom, Badda Bing, and Find Your Inner Mobster

## Jon Macks

simon & schuster
new york london toronto sydney singapore

*SIMON & SCHUSTER*

*Rockefeller Center*

*1230 Avenue of the Americas*

*New York, NY 10020*

*Designed by Karolina Harris*

PHOTO CREDITS: *page 21, top:* Corbis; *page 21, bottom:* Corbis; *page 39, top:*
AP/Wide World Photos; *page 39, bottom:* AP/Wide World Photos; *page 64, top:*
AP/Wide World Photos; *page 64, bottom:* AP/Wide World Photos; *page 69:*
© Wes Thompson/The Stock Market; *page 70, top:* © Richard Berenholtz/The
Stock Market; *page 70, bottom, house:* © Blaine Harrington/The Stock Market;
*page 70, bottom, yard art:* © Bob Schatz.

*Manufactured in the United States of America*

*10  9  8  7  6  5  4  3  2  1*

*Library of Congress Cataloging-in-Publication Data is available.*

*ISBN 0-7432-0471-9*

# Acknowledgments

To David Rosenthal and Marysue Rucci at Simon & Schuster, who served as my Godfather and Consigliere in the creation and writing of this book. I wrote it because they made me an offer I couldn't refuse . . . money;

To Jack Dytman, Bob Myman, and Mike Klein, who handle my money;

To Jay Leno, Billy Crystal, James Carville, David Steinberg, Whoopi Goldberg, Don Mischer, Lou Horvitz, Michael Seligman, John Moffitt, Pat Lee, Herb Kohl, Tom Bergeron, Jimmy Brogan, Bruce Vilanch, George Schlatter, and to all the people who have ever encouraged and inspired me;

To Alexander Fleming, for discovering penicillin;

To Tony Vanella, Alex SantaBarbara, Dave Esola, Bob Caruso, Moch, Fang, Doug Warrick, and all the guys I grew up with who helped me develop an appreciation for the street and its colorful language;

To Saddam Hussein and Florida Secretary of State Katherine Harris. I often picture both of them naked;

To the teams I was lucky enough to help coach this year—the Agoura Lightning baseball team, the Kickin' Coyotes Soccer team, and the Agoura Sixth Grade Girls Travel Basketball Team;

To all the writers at "The Tonight Show" and "Hollywood Squares";

To Miss October;

To my parents, my brother Adam; his wife, Susan, and new baby, Jeremy;

To the Burbank Pilots, my fourth L.A. Thirty-Plus Baseball team in three years. It would be remiss of me not to mention my .483 average this year. Hitting and fielding;

And finally, to former President Bill Clinton, without whom the past eight years of comedy would not be the same.

*to Julie, Daniel, Samantha, and Ricky*

# Introduction

The Mafia, like Amway and clog dancing, is a way of life. But sadly, it is a way of life that has been dying out. According to the 2000 U.S. Census, there are only five actual members of the mob left in the United States.*

*For some reason, the number five has always been important when it comes to the Mafia. There were five great mob families: the Gambinos, the Genoveses, the Bonannos, the Colombos, and the Luccheses; and there are five great mob movies: *Godfather 1, Godfather 2, Analyze This, Once Upon a Time in America,* and *Goodfellas.* Some movie critics would put *Scarface* on this list instead of *Analyze This.* Let's just say those movie critics are going to end up with two broken thumbs up. *Analyze This* is on the list because it is one of the funniest movies of all time, Billy Crystal is a friend, it has DeNiro, and finally, Al Pacino, who was in *Scarface,* must be punished for agreeing to do *Godfather 3.*

What happened? What went wrong? How did one of America's great economic engines crash and burn faster than a Ford Explorer on a set of Firestone tires? Some would blame the federal government. Others attribute the decline to RICO. Still others point to the Mafia's unusually high mortality rate.* But the truth is, the real problem is that the old-timers are dying out and there is no one to replace them. And just as important, there is no one willing to take the time to teach those who want to join the mob about the Mafia way of life.

I know, I know, some of you would say that the mob dying out is a good thing. Here are five reasons why you are wrong. Thanks to the mob:

1. Grown men who don't play professional ball still get to use baseball bats. Which personally brings back so many great baseball memories from childhood, of going down to the park with Dad and whacking some guy over the head.
2. The modern mob is one of America's great equal opportunity employers. There is a Jewish Mafia, a Russian Mafia, an Italian Mafia, an African-American Mafia, and an Asian Mafia.† A president

---

*Average life expectancy of a woman in an organized crime family: 109.2 years; average life expectancy of a man in an organized crime family: 23.1 years.

†And before any of you get upset and think this book focuses on people whose last name ends in a vowel, just stop being so god-

of the United States has been sued for sexual harassment, Denny's has been accused of racial discrimination, but to this day, there has never been one successful EEOC complaint filed against the mob.

3. Thanks to mob movies, we have Robert DeNiro.
4. Without mob funerals, the floral industry would be bankrupt.
5. Without the mob, no one would have ever heard of the late Abe Vigoda.

So think of the mob as an endangered species, and just like with any endangered species, active steps need to be taken to ensure that this valuable cross-section of Americana is around for generations to come. That is the purpose of this book, to serve as an introduction, a sort of Mafia 101. And much like a college course, it is organized to help you walk through the entire mob way of life.

Chapter 1 is about the **Mob Cultural Experience,** what The Life is all about. Think of it as the background information you will need in order to under-

damned politically correct. I am writing about the mob, organized crime, a great way of life that has opened the door to people of every religion, race, ethnic group, color, or creed. Back in a time when law firms, country clubs, and colleges were excluding Jews, the American mob opened its doors and let in people named Lansky and Siegel. And let's be honest, there are more African Americans in the Mafia than in the cast of "Friends." Case closed.

stand your conversion. It features mob fashion, the language of the mob, culinary delights, and the rich cultural life that awaits you.

Chapter 2 deals with **Looking and Acting Like a Mob Guy.**

Chapter 3 features ways of **Making a Living** in the mob.

Chapter 4 focuses on your **Other Family,** taking you from cradle to early grave as we describe the great mob circle of life.

Chapter 5 centers on the **Retirement Years.**

Chapter 6 is the final section before the big test, with real-life stories that can open the mob heart and kindle the mob spirit in the section we call **Minestrone for the Mob Soul.**

Chapter 7 is the **Mob Final Exam,** the test that will determine whether you enter The Life or whether we end yours.

The final chapters of the book take you through the top-secret mob initiation ceremony and provide you with the Racketeer's Pledge.*

Many chapters end with a quiz. I cannot emphasize enough the importance of passing these tests. It is only by doing well on them that you can qualify for The Life.

And one final note before you turn the page and begin your entry into the world of the mob. This book is the definitive guide on how to become a **twenty-**

*The mob equivalent of the doctor's Hippocratic Oath.

**first-century mobster.** We've taken the old-world values and rules and updated them for the information age. This is not for Mustache Petes or *gavones* from the street. This book is for hotshot professional college grads, young men and women who want the challenges of a well-respected, lucrative career without having to put up with those assholes getting their MBA.

So best of luck as you begin your journey. May you live a hundred years and may you never have a three-hundred-pound cellmate named Bubba.

*This life of ours, this is a wonderful life. If you can get through life like this and get away with it, hey that's great. But it's very unpredictable. There are so many ways you can screw it up.*

—The late Paul Castellano

# 1

## The Mob Cultural Experience

A people is defined by its culture.
**—Margaret Mead**
I first grew penicillin mold in a culture.
**—Alexander Fleming**

This is not a Fodor's guide to Italy. For years, people equated the mob with Italians. Wrong wrong wrong. There is a Jewish mob, a Russian mob, an Asian mob, a Black mob, and the scariest one of all: the Mormon mob—with their charging everyone 10 percent, having four wives, and dispatching their enforcer "Little" Jimmy Osmond.

The point is, being a wiseguy isn't about *who* you are or *where* you're from or even *what* you do for a living. Being a wiseguy is a unique way of living. It's also a unique way of dying, usually involving an ice pick, a chair, and duct tape. But let's skip that for now. Let's concentrate on all the good things about living as a Mafioso and take a look at the sophisticated world of mob culture.

# Mob Fashion: How to Look Like a Million While Stealing a Million

The well-dressed mobster of the 1970s is an anachronism in the year 2001. Frilly tuxedo shirts are out; however, there are a few items of fashion that never go out of style:

Gold chains
Bulletproof vests
Mustaches

This is true for both mob men and mob women, although as general observation, the mustaches of the men tend not to be as coarse and heavy.

If you want to look like a mob guy, you don't want to look like a tourist from North Dakota. So the rule is simple: black suit, white shirt from Memorial Day to Labor Day; black suit, black shirt from Labor Day till the end of May. If you want to be a success, you have to dress for success and act like a success. There is only one other rule: Never go outside without your pinky ring. Now it's time for your first test. See if you can pick out which one of the people in these photos is a mob guy.

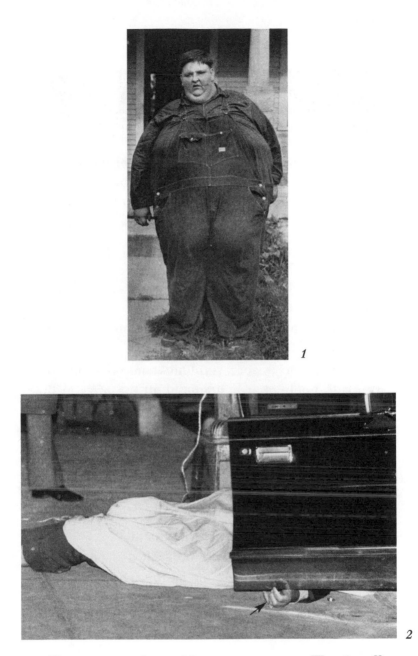

If you guessed guy #2 you are correct. The tip-off:
He was wearing a pinky ring.

# The Traditional Nicknames of the Mob

But just looking like a mob guy can only get you so far in life. Basically, it can get you first place in the Joe Pesci lookalike contest or a nice table at a restaurant. But to be a real member of the mob—or what is called a "made guy"*—you need to take step #1: acquire that all-important nickname. For a nickname is not just a means of identification, it's a way of telling the world that you belong, that you are part of a rich and vibrant culture. And remember, it is only with a nickname that you will be allowed in next October's scheduled "Million Mobster March."

The best way to get a good nickname is to pick one yourself. Look what happens to all the guys in that other organized criminal activity, major league baseball. They get stuck with whatever stupid nickname Chris Berman gives them. Like Randy "Big Unit" Johnson. Sorry, the only big unit in my book is John C. Holmes. Okay, maybe Tommy Lee, if you think that home video wasn't special effects. So never let another mob guy give you a nickname.

Here's what to do. On your first day on the job, right after reporting in and getting changed in the locker room, go to roll call and when the capo calls out your name, announce real loud that back home,

*Which is not to be confused with the other type of "made guy"—the one who can usually be found shopping at Ikea.

they call you "Handsome Marvin." Otherwise, you end up with a nickname like Big Pussy. Which coincidentally was Roseanne's college nickname.

Here's another good nickname to try: "Tony the Horse." If people call you that, every woman in town will think you're hung like frigging Man o' War.

What happens if you don't do what I say? Then somebody who doesn't like you is going to give you a nickname, and these nicknames tend to be about obvious things. Like Jewish wiseguys are always called "the Jew," or if you're politically correct, "the Hebrew." And if three thousand senior citizens in Palm Beach hadn't been in such a hurry to get to the early bird special last election day, at least one Jew would have been called Mr. Vice President.* Guys with big noses are called "Noz." Guys who aren't well equipped are called "Needledick." These are not names you want to answer to.

To help you out, here is a list of nicknames to avoid:

Gefilte Fish
Stinky Finger
The Episcopalian
The Dancer
Sweetlips
Quick on the Trigger and We Don't Mean
  With a Gun

*Although being called Mr. Vice President is more demeaning than being called "Jewboy."

## Famous Nicknames
## of Mobsters

See if you can match the mobsters with their nicknames

| | | |
|---|---|---|
| 1. Al Capone | a. The Enforcer |
| 2. Frank Nitti | b. Stainmaster |
| 3. Benjamin Siegel | c. Scarface |
| 4. Bill Clinton | d. Bugsy |
| 5. Joe Valachi | e. Old One Nut |
| 6. Louis Lepke | f. Amortization Arnold |
| 7. Mickey Cohen | g. The yid with the id |
| 8. Arnold Turkowitz | |

• • • • • • • • • • • • • • • • • • • • • • • • • • • • • • • •

The correct answers are: 1–c, 2–a, 3–d, 4–b, 5–e, 6 and 7–g (note—both Cohen and Lepke were strict Freudians, thus the shared nickname), 8–f (Turkowitz was the first accountant to the mob. He is considered the father of the illegal business deduction; he is also credited with coming up with the concept of declaring cops on the take as "dependents.")

At this point some of you may wonder why Bill Clinton is listed under the genus "mobster." It is because, as Darwin would say, he had all three attributes of a mobster.

Typical mobster: always being targeted by demented federal prosecutors

Bill Clinton: always being targeted by demented federal prosecutors

Typical mobster: involved in shady deals
Bill Clinton: Whitewater

Typical mobster: cigar in mouth, mistress on the side
Bill Clinton: cigar in mistress

Thus we come to the inescapable conclusion that Bill Clinton is a member of America's only true remaining crime family.

## The Language of the Mob

You can't just walk the walk. You must also talk the talk. Because if you act *and* talk like a mob guy, you will be a mob guy. It doesn't matter how great your nickname is, if you sound like Melvin from Great Neck, it ain't gonna fly. So here is the only guide you will ever need to learn how to talk like a wiseguy.

The Golden Rule: There are two basic topics of mob conversation—sex and murder. And there are five hundred different ways to communicate that you want to have sex or kill someone, or have sex, then kill someone. Master a few of these terms of art, sprinkle them in your conversations, and everyone will know you are a man of respect.

That's it, that's all you need to know. You don't need to learn Yiddish, Italian, or Russian. Just use the following everyday words and phrases in conversation:

- **Words and Phrases That Indicate a Sexual Act or Body Part**
Playing off the fairway
*Mangia la pesca*
Slipping the old cannoli
Diving like a Don King fighter
Slipping the old sauseech
Licking the boot of Italy
Carpet cleaning
Shtupping
Hung like the Leaning Tower of Pisa
Sun-ripened tomatoes
Entering the Lincoln Tunnel
Going down like an Internet stock
Widow duty
Raising a fine piece of veal
Cleaning the shankbone
Playing with the little godfather
Paying the man some respect
Making the *capo di tutti capi* an offer he can't refuse
Seventy ('cause real men don't do 69)
Taking a trip down the Garden State Parkway
Eating at the Meadowlands
Dining al fresco
Meet Mr. Lansky
Doing hard time
Dancing to the accordion
Illegally paving the interstate
Seeing the sixth family
Having a little anti-pasta
Tenderizing some beef

Sticking the osso bucco into the oven
Giving it the old FBI (frigging big instrument)
Playing hide the pepperoni
Eating clams casino
Cigar dipping
Making the pasta firm
Inserting tab A into slot B
Cleaning the plumbing
Hitting on Twenty-one
Coppola-ing a feel
Badda bing badda boom
Uncorking the bat
Spray-painting with DNA
Leaving a trail of DNA evidence
Nonkosher porking
Stuffing some prosciutto
Cloving the garlic
Making her an offer she can't refuse
Taking it into the end zone (not what you think,
   you sick bastards)
Packing a piece
Carrying heat
Unloading a set of 38s

• **Words and Phrases That Indicate
Killing Someone**
Whack job
Sending them to meet the *capo di tutti capi*
New Jersey population control
Visiting the landfill
Making fertilizer

Paying the ultimate vig
Sending a guy a message without using Western
    Union
Sleeping with the fishes
Sleeping with the crabs (which is different from
    getting the crabs)
Going on a lead diet
Playing catch with a lead baseball
Having a meeting with Mr. Smith and Mr. Wesson
Giving a coronary
Getting reservations at the dining room in Hell
Kissing the cement
Vacationing permanently in a hot place
NFL'ing them
Tenderizing some meat
Sending them to the big bocce hall in the sky
Investing in flower shops
Ending their smoking problem
Taking them for a swim
Fitting them for a new pair of shoes
Celebrating St. Valentine's early this year
Performing involuntary nonelective surgery

There are only five phrases other than the above that you will ever need to use in conversation. At one point, Simon & Schuster considered publishing a "Mob-English, English-Mob" dictionary until mob linguistics experts advised them that the only other phrases the average Mafia guy needs are:

BROTHER-IN-LAW: someone sleeping with your wife
GAVONE: an uncouth lout

GOING TO THE MATTRESSES: I'll give you a hint, it doesn't
  mean having sex
MUFFIN: a woman whose name you don't know who
  you want to have sex with
PLEA BARGAIN: no explanation necessary

Now let's see how a typical conversation between two mob guys would go. "Vinny" has a date, but "Murray" is enlisting his help to rub out someone who has wronged him.

VINNY: What youse* doing tonight, looking for some muffin?

MURRAY: Nah, I got to go see the guy who turns out to be my brother-in-law. I need your help taking him to visit the landfill. And his capo can't find out or we'll end up going to the mattresses.

VINNY: I can't. I need to deliver some of the old cannoli. I'm spending too much time meeting Mr. Lansky all by myself.

MURRAY: Rumor has it all you do is eat at the Meadowlands. And the Meadowlands will still be a swamp at midnight. We gotta introduce our former business associate to the *capo di tutti capi.*

VINNY: If I don't do a little widow duty, I'm goin' to have my own whack job.

MURRAY: Before you help a widow, you gotta make a widow.

*Never forget the one and only rule of grammar: Begin a sentence with the word *youse* only if it's something like "youse guys are frigging dead."

VINNY: Where did you hear that crap about me goin' to the Meadowlands? What, you think I need to carpet clean? All I do is drive through the Lincoln Tunnel.

MURRAY: Well, stop actin' like a *gavone*, drive through the Lincoln Tunnel and help me send this guy to the Meadowlands, then you can go play hide the pepperoni.

Notice that in the above conversation, many of the phrases are interchangeable.

## Mob Cuisine

Dining in the Mafia is very simple. You can eat regular or you can eat "light."

*Regular dinner:* cicoria insalata (dandelion salad), shrimp scampi appetizer, baked pork chops, pasta e fagioli, garlic bread, clams calamari, veal milanese, steak Sinatra, two shots of grappa, a bottle of Chianti Classico, manicotti marinara, mussels in a light sauce, and lemon granita.

*Eating light:* Same as above but skip the cicoria insalata because the dandelions can give you gas.

Since approximately 50 percent of one's time in the mob is spent eating or killing people in restaurants, some of you may decide to save money on dining out by opening your own place. Personally, I think it's too much work for the up-and-coming professional. If you're going to work that hard, you might as well go legit and run a real restaurant. For those who have their heart set on running a restaurant, here is an easy way to tell the difference between running a legitimate restaurant and a mob restaurant:

Legitimate restaurant: You make reservations to eat there.
Mob restaurant: You have reservations about eating there when you see the dead guy in the men's room.

Legitimate restaurant: When you walk in you see specials written on a chalk blackboard.
Mob restaurant: When you walk in you see a body outline chalked on the floor.

Legitimate restaurant: Today's veal was yesterday's calf.
Mob restaurant: Today's "veal" finished last yesterday in the seventh race at Belmont.

Legitimate restaurant: Lobster is shipped in frozen from Maine.
Mob restaurant: Louie is shipped out frozen in dry ice.

Legitimate restaurant: Loud banging is a busy chef in the back.
Mob restaurant: Loud banging involves Fredo and two cocktail waitresses or it means the bouncer forgot to use a silencer.

Legitimate restaurant: There's a fly in your soup.
Mob restaurant: Some guy's eye is in your soup.

Legitimate restaurant: Food critics give it four stars.
Mob restaurant: Food critics didn't see nothin'.

Legitimate restaurant: You end a great meal with a flaming dessert.
Mob restaurant: You end a bad year by setting the place on fire.

Legitimate restaurant: People are packed in.
Mob restaurant: People are packing heat.

## Entertainment

There's nothing worth doing since Frank died. Stay at home and get drunk watching *Ocean's 11*.

Actually, there are a few things you can do to while away your free time. Like going on a mob cultural excursion.

## Mob Cultural Excursion

The great thing about being in the Mafia is that there are no conference calls (the lines could be tapped), no bringing your work home with you (who wants to bring a corpse to the house), and no punching a time clock. Punching out a guy behind on his vig, sure, but no punching a clock. Which leaves you plenty of time to take the family on a cultural excursion, otherwise known in the civilian world as a vacation.

## Las Vegas

Las Vegas claims it is now family-friendly, but it's always been family-friendly—especially if you were in one of the five families. There are two types of people who go to Las Vegas—high rollers and tourists. Clearly you want to be a high roller. And here's a simple quiz to see if you have what it takes.

### High-Roller Quiz

1. Your idea of a show is
   a. Spending $5,000 for two tickets to see Streisand
   b. Asking the hotel concierge for "comps" so you can see the Bobby Berosini orangutans

2. The dealer is showing a six, you have two eights, you
   a. Get a marker for $50,000, split the eights, and let it ride
   b. Tell the dealer you don't have any eights and say "Go fish"

3. A typical night involves
   a. Three hookers in a hot tub, Charlie Sheen, and a bottle of Dom
   b. Dry-humping your wife's leg while she's asleep

4. You're on first-name basis with every
   a. Pit boss and madam in town
   b. The cashier at the 99-cent buffet

5. You spend the afternoon
   a. Paying $2,000 to an escort named Candy for a "Hoover" special
   b. Actually visiting the Hoover dam

· · · · · · · · · · · · · · · · · · · · · · · · · · · · · · · · · · · · ·

If you answered "a" to every question, you're a high roller. If you answered "b" to any question, you're a tourist. High rollers are mob guys; tourists are mob meat. But not all mob guys are high rollers. Those who don't make the grade go to . . .

## Atlantic City

Atlantic City—A.C., which stands for "always crappy." You know you're a loser if that's your idea of a gambling vacation. It is, however, only one of two places in New Jersey where a mob guy will ever be found. The other is buried in the end zone at the Meadowlands.

That pretty much takes you through the rich culture of The Life. But before you learn how to look and act like a mobster, we have to make sure you are qualified to graduate.

### Test One: Culture

1. The Last Supper is
   a. Something painted by DaVinci
   b. Closing time at the Stardust $3.99 steak-and-shrimp dinner
   c. The name of a restaurant in Brooklyn

2. A good nickname for a guy who cuts people with a knife is
   a. O.J.
   b. The Mohel
   c. Stiletto Johnny

3. The proper way to ask a young woman if she wants sex is to
   a. Ask if she would like to have a mutually con-sensual act of oral sex*
   b. Marry her
   c. Tell her you once said hi to Joe Pesci (chicks love that pickup line)

• • • • • • • • • • • • • • • • • • • • • • • • • • • • • • • • • •

Okay, that was your first test. If you answered "c" to all of the above, congratulations, you are ready to move on. If you broke into my office, stole the answers, and got them all right, you can skip ahead to Chapter 6. If you answered "a" or "b" to any of the above, I'd tell you to shoot yourself but it's a waste of a bullet. Let's just say that every mob family has a Fredo.

*Hint: "a" is obviously incorrect. Mafia guys just don't do that. And anyone who ever says they do is a liar.

*Editor's Note:* According to the Kinsey report on sex and organized crime figures, men and women in the Mafia are just as likely as anyone else to perform oral sex. They just hate talking about it. Or, in mob-speak, they take the Fifth when it comes to 69.

## 2

# Looking and Acting Like a Mob Guy

What doth the Lord require of thee,
but to do justly, love mercy, and walk
humbly with thy God?
                          **—Micah 6:8**

The informant voluntarily took a walk
out the window of a ten-story building.
                          **—Abe "Kid Twist" Reles**

## Walk Like a Mob Guy

Mob guys don't walk, they strut. Look at Sonny Corleone . . . right away you could tell he was in the mob. Slobodan Milosevic . . . has the swagger of a hit man. Now look at Richard Simmons . . . he just radiates "not a mob guy."

Here is a good way to practice at home. Stand in front of the mirror, one hand on the button of your jacket, like you're about to reach for a piece. The other hand is bouncing up and down and moving side to side like you're either a spastic or a middleweight throwing a punch. Your head should be swinging around like Linda Blair or the world's greatest hooker. Put a bounce in your step like there are hot coals on the sidewalk. And most important, if anyone makes fun of the way you walk, simply walk over to them and bounce your knee directly into their groinal area.

## Smoke Like a Mob Guy

Mob guys have to smoke the right way. I know what you're thinking: "But Jon, tobacco is bad because it kills people." As the late great Philip Morris once said, "It is better to die coughing on your feet than live healthy on your knees." The most important tip about smoking is not to hold a cigarette like you're some kind of cell-phone Eurotrash. The way to tell the difference is this: Eurotrash hold their filtered clove cigarettes between their thumb and index fingers; mob guys who have been in The Life more than three years don't have an index finger. That's why if you want to look like a made guy, smoke a cigar and keep it in your mouth.

What about secondhand smoke? As a general rule, the mob does not really respect nonsmokers' rights, so you are pretty much on your own if someone else's smoke is annoying. A good suggestion is this: If the offending smoker is higher up on the organization chart than you are, consider it an honor to inhale his nicotine cloud; if he's lower on the organization chart than you, tell him to either snuff out the cigarette or you'll snuff *him* out.

One final note: If you see a lot of smoke pouring out of a mob guy's Lincoln, that means either his car or his head is on fire.

## Transportation

There are some who would argue that a mob car is part of the culture and would belong in Chapter 1. Like my editor. But I forgot to put it in there and now it's stuck here in Chapter 2. As my mother would say, don't have a conniption over it. There are children starving in West Virginia, do you think they care? They're so hungry they probably ate Chapter 1. Anyway, I digress. What you need to know is that driving the right set of wheels is very important to looking the part. This (opposite) should make it easy.

## Kiss Like a Mob Guy

The rules are simple: Only kiss guys. And each kiss has a different meaning.
1. If you kiss a man on both hands, it is a sign of respect.
2. If you kiss a man on both cheeks, it is a sign you will soon betray him.
3. If you kiss a man on the mouth with a light danc-

FIRST CAR

LAST CAR

ing of the tongue against his teeth, probing until there is a small opening and then inserting it with a teasing thrust until you hear a slight moan of ecstasy, it either means you are a huge Bette Midler fan or I should start writing romance novels.

Do you really want to kiss a woman? You never really know where that mouth has been. *Capisce?* Who knows which end of the pistol the cocktail waitress was cleaning. So you kiss close family members because they're family, and you kiss not-so-close family members because they're about to be sleeping with the fish.

## Grooming Like a Mob Guy

Mob guys never look like slobs. That's how you could tell John Gotti wasn't a real plumber. Real plumbers don't wear $2,000 Armani suits; they wear Kmart specials and black socks with sneakers. And amazingly, it only took the Feds fifteen years and a $16 million investigation to figure out that Mr. Gotti maybe had an additional source of income.

### Things Mob Guys Will Need to Ensure Perfect Grooming

- A toothpick for cleaning and to chew on
  This is essential for both dental hygiene and for jamming up under someone's fingernails in the unlikely event there are no bamboo shoots lying around

- Pomade or BrylCream for the hair
  In an emergency, Quaker State 10W30 will work.
  This is critical because usually, when you're pho-
  tographed, everyone can see your hair because
  your hat is being used to hide your face. If you
  are in doubt as to how much to use, try to remember this formula: In the *R* months, never
  wear more hair oil than Jerry Lewis.
- The name of a twenty-four-hour manicurist
  Not for your nails. All manicurists are easy.
- Nail clippers
  Clipping one's nails is a great way to pass the
  time while acting unconcerned during a lengthy
  grand jury arraignment.

## Things Mob Girls Will Need to Ensure Perfect Grooming

- Chewing gum and a toothpick
  Chewing gum for proper dental hygiene, a
  toothpick because you will need someplace hy-
  gienic on which to store your chewing gum during sex.
- Hairspray, lots of it
  Enough hairspray to cause polar bears to die
  from sunburn because of the hole in the ozone.
- A twenty-four-hour manicurist
  Not for your nails, you're wearing Lee press-ons.
  Manicurists are great because they listen and tell
  no one. They are the priests of the cosmetology
  industry.

- Nail clippers
  Because grand juries just aren't for men anymore—see nail clippers in section on grooming
  tips for men.

## Hairstyles

Don't kid yourself, *size does matter*, but only with women's hair. The bigger the better. The blonder the better. Think of Anna Nicole Smith as the perfect mob woman. In fact, I bet she could have whacked that ninety-year-old—smothered that baby with . . . never mind, I drifted.

Men's hair should be short. Blond hair should only be an option when going into the witness protection program.

## Giving Good Phone

If you're going to act like a mob guy, you have to know how to give good phone. Mob guys do not talk on cell phones. Mob guys do not have those silly little Nextel yuppie phones. Mob guys do not use phones at home for outgoing calls. Home phones are used to make book or when one of your soldiers is letting you know the hit has gone down. Mob guys only use safe pay phones. Plus mob guys do not wipe off the receiver with Clorox disinfectant wipes *before* they talk because they're worried about germs. They wipe off the phone *afterward* because of fingerprints.

• • •

That's it, you have finished Chapter 2 and should know how to look and act like a mobster. But, as the great Vito Corleone said about Carlo Rizzi, Before we give you your living, we have to make sure you pass your test.

## Test at the End of Chapter 2

1. The first thing to look for in a restaurant is
   a. A good wine list
   b. To make sure the kosher chef really keeps two sets of dishes
   c. One of those old-fashioned toilets that you can hide a gun behind so if you have to send Michael in there, he doesn't come out with just his dick in his hand

2. Tony Dogs sees you on the street. He kisses you on each cheek. That means
   a. His Viagra has just kicked in
   b. You better start wearing a bra because he thinks you're a woman
   c. Duck!

3. Walking into a room with a swagger and then pacing back and forth is a sign of
   a. Burning, itching, and swelling
   b. Too much Starbucks coffee
   c. That you have the walk of a mob guy

4. Mob guys never go swimming in the ocean because
   a. Their hair oil is an environmental hazard
   b. The average mob guy is so fat that Greenpeace will circle to try and protect him
   c. You never want to show disrespect to a sacred mob burial ground

5. Toothpicks are for
   a. Dental hygiene
   b. Storing gum during sex
   c. Stabbing out an informant's eye
   d. All of the above

• • • • • • • • • • • • • • • • • • • • • • • • • • • • • • • • • • •

SCORING

Give yourself 3 points for each "c" answer and a bonus 4 points if you answered "d" on question 5.

14–16 points: You are a wiseguy in training. You scored better than Charlie Sheen at a hooker convention.

11–12: You have promise.

9–10: Go back and review before moving on to Chapter 3.

8 and under: Have you thought about a career in telemarketing?

# 3
## Making a Living

Man may work from sun to sun
But a woman's work is never done.
**—Anonymous**

You call that work? Sitting there and writing
this filth. What's wrong with you? Law school
wasn't good enough for Mr. Comedy Writer.
He has time to write a book but can't find
three minutes to call his mother.
**—Sylvia Macks, author's mother**

There **are** three basic career paths for the mobster who wants to make a nice living: upper management, middle management, and the exciting new world of the high-tech mob. But before we explore those career opportunities, we must start with the basics, the tools of the trade.

## Tools of the Trade

A carpenter needs his hammer, a surgeon needs a scalpel, a landscaper needs a chain saw, and to live the mob lifestyle, a Mafia member needs . . . well, actually, he also needs a hammer, scalpel, and chain saw. But in addition he needs three basic tools of the trade: a black Lincoln town car, ready mix cement, and a baseball bat.

## The Lincoln

You need a big car for a variety of reasons. For one thing, it's a penis substitute. Let's be honest—the big cigars, the big guns, the powerful cars . . . they're all a cry for help.

However, in addition to the big car being phallic compensation, it is also an integral part of the job. You need a big engine for fast getaways, you need a roomy backseat to hide in during a toll-booth hit, and you need a big trunk to store, albeit temporarily, informants.

## Ready Mix Cement

The ready mix cement is important for what is called in the trade a "permanent shoe fitting." This way, you can clear out the above-mentioned inform-ant from the trunk of your Lincoln while providing a wonderful artificial reef for the East River aquatic life.

## Baseball Bat

This is the most important piece of equipment you can have. Walk down the street with a gun and people get suspicious. Walk down the street in your sweatpants holding a baseball bat and people think you just came from a company softball game. And in a way, it helps lessen guilt. With a bat you don't have to think of yourself as a cold-blooded killer. Think of yourself as a designated hitter.

## The Big Debate:
## Metal versus Wooden Bats

The old-timers insist on using wooden bats. I say it's time for the mob's greatest hitters to join the twenty-first century. Wooden bats can splinter; they tend to be heavy; and in a time of high overhead and cost-cutting, the need to constantly replace wooden bats can wreak havoc on a budget. Three good solid hits and a wood bat is worthless. That's why I like the metal bats. They're long-lasting, plus with the new lightweight titanium—I particularly like the Omaha TPX and the Easton Z-core—you can generate greater bat speed and not get jammed on an inside body part. Can you imagine Capone with a metal bat and today's training methods? He would have hit 75 in one season.

## Upper Management:
## The Two Big Positions

The good news: Because of a relatively high turnover rate in the mob the past few years, there are a lot of upper-level management job openings for bright young men and women who have what it takes to survive the rat race.*

*Richard Hatch of "Survivor" is the perfect guy to be a mob boss. He is cunning, manipulative, treacherous, plus he knows what to do with rats.

Which brings us to the two most important positions in any mob family: undertaker and dermatologist. No, that was a joke. It's florist and cannoli maker. Another joke for the insiders. Everyone knows it's the Godfather and Consigliere.

## Godfather

What a great job title. Is there a Jewish mother out there who wouldn't be proud to call her friends and say "my son the Godfather"?* It's a hell of a lot better than "my son the doctor." Not only do Godfathers make more money than doctors, they don't have that annoying messiah complex. The only difference is that the average doctor ends up killing more people than the average Godfather. Especially the ones at HMOs, but that's for another book.

The problem for those of you who want to become a Godfather is that the Mafia rarely promotes from within. Usually, to become Godfather, you need to start your own family, a time-consuming and often unsuccessful enterprise, or you need to begin what in the corporate business world is called a "hostile takeover." In other words, you need to whack the guy ahead of you in the food chain.

Now, for those of you who are squeamish about

---

*Think about it. Louis "Lepke" Buchalter, a Jew, was head of Murder Inc. back in the 1930s. Yet a Jew wasn't picked as a vice presidential nominee until the year 2000. The Mafia is less restricted than the Democratic Party.

that, let me point out that this is not much different from what happens in the real business world every day. I'll prove it: For the word *Godfather* in the next paragraph, substitute the word *CEO.*

First the Godfather is given an exit interview where a number of his longtime associates initiate a discussion of the issue of severance.* If the longtime Godfather refuses to voluntarily step down, which is invariably the case, he is taken out for a final "surprise" retirement dinner, there are several shots in his honor, and his retirement is then prominently featured in the *New York Post.*

If you followed these steps, congratulations, you are the new Godfather. *Cent' Anni!*

But this brings us to the next section: How to Get Rid of the Godfather.

## New and Unique Ways to Whack Somebody in the New Millennium

A restaurant hit is the traditional way to become Godfather. However, that is going the way of the wooden bat. Because for the "everything must be new or it's no good" Internet generation, there are a number of cre-

---

*Mafia severance is a bit different from the usual two weeks' notice at IBM. Mafia severance usually starts with severing the thumbs, then the feet, and occasionally the "little godfather." See the *Valachi Papers.*

ative ways to ensure that there is a job opening waiting for you at the top. Here are five unique ways to have your Godfather go visit the big family in the sky.

- Once he turns fifty, take him in for the colonoscopy from Hell.
- Exploding bocce balls.
- Hire someone to do it cheap on Priceline.
- Get him hooked on Krispy Kreme doughnuts. Remember what the dealers say, first batch is free.
- Switch the lane signs in the Lincoln Tunnel.

All of these will result in slow or instant death.

But what exactly is it that you do once you become a Godfather? What is the job description? It's actually rather simple: You whack people before they whack you and you make people offers they can't refuse. That doesn't mean cold calling them on the phone and offering them a great deal on a no-load mutual fund. An offer they can't refuse means that you persuade them to do something that is in your financial interest and in their long-term health interest.

Let's be honest, if you are joining the modern Mafia, you can't do the "horse's head" bit. The last thing you want is for both the FBI and PETA to come after you. At least you can reason with the FBI. No, it's much better in this day and age to use nonlethal methods of persuasion. Especially for you college grads—either confuse him with references to Sartre proving that he does not exist or give him an atomic wedgie.*

*But watch the sexual harassment lawsuit.

## Consigliere

Consigliere: (noun) Trusted adviser, counselor, rabbi, mentor. The voice of reason and strategic advice.

If the Godfather can be compared to a doctor, then the Consigliere can be compared to a lawyer. He is more than just the number two man in a Mafia family. He is often the one who survives after the Godfather gets whacked. So in making your career choice, you may decide it is better to rust than to burn out.

The role of Consigliere is a valued one—Don Corleone had Genco Abbadando, Michael had Tom Hagen, Conan O'Brien had Andy Richter. But remember, a Consigliere is your adviser, not your mouthpiece. Your mouthpiece is your criminal defense lawyer or a cheap hooker. To see if you have what it takes to be a Consigliere, take a look at these everyday life situations and see if you would have the courage and wisdom to give the same advice.

- A Consigliere would have told Jesus, "The guy who sets up the meeting, Judas, that's the traitor."
- A Consigliere would have told Abe Lincoln, "Why are you going to a musical at Ford's theater? You just won the war. Tell the wife to go by herself."
- A Consigliere would have told Pharaoh, "This Moses guy is nothing but trouble, let him go. And if you chase him, wear a life jacket."
- A Consigliere would have told Bill Clinton, "Dump the fat broad and date someone who is not mentally irregular. And clean up the evi-

dence. No sane person leaves a date wearing her man's love grappa."

- A Consigliere would have told JFK, "You pissed off Fidel, you pissed off Momo, you pissed off the Traficantes, don't ride around in a convertible."
- A Consigliere would have told Princess Di, "Never get in a car driven by a guy with an empty six-pack in the front seat."
- A Consigliere would have told Ron Goldman, "She's a broad, let her come back and get her own frigging sunglasses."
- A Consigliere would have told Liberace, "Don't let anyone go the wrong way on an exit, *capisce?*"
- A Consigliere would have told Woody Allen, "Are you nuts? It's an *infamata* marrying your own daughter."
- A Consigliere would have told John Gotti, "You ever notice that Sammy the Bull is taking a lot of notes?"
- A Consigliere would have told Rudy Giuliani, "The next time you get a picture taken, wear a hat."
- A Consigliere would have told Mama Cass, "Try the soup, I hear the ham on rye is terrible."
- A Consigliere would have told Tom Hagen that a horse should not be in someone's bed, the same thing a Consigliere would have told Catherine the Great.
- A Consigliere would have told defense lawyer

Alan Dershowitz, "Shut up. Every time you open your stupid mouth, it makes people anti-Semitic. You are bad for the Jews."

If you would have given these people the same advice, you have what it takes to be a Consigliere or to work on the Psychic Hotline.

How can you tell whether you are better suited to be a Godfather or a Consigliere? Simple, by taking the following one-question test, which, interestingly, also appeared in last May's issue of *Cosmopolitan,* under the title "How to Get That Godfather to Propose and 15 Tips to a Bigger Orgasm." By the way, tip #1: Date a guy with a big tip.

## Job Aptitude Test

Solazzo comes to you with a deal. He proposes that he handle the distribution and marketing, you handle protection. For that you get 40 percent.

- If you immediately accept the deal after demanding 50 percent, you have what it takes to be a mob Godfather.
- If you ask him "distribution and marketing of what, you never said what the hell it is we're selling," you have what it takes to become a mob Consigliere.
- If you ask "40 percent of the net or gross?," you have what it takes to be a mob accountant.
- If you say "Tataglia is a pimp. He never would have had the brains to kill Santino. The man behind this is Barzini," then you have what it takes to be a mob novelist.
- And if you notice that Solazzo has a really tight butt, you will really enjoy prison.

But what if you've gotten halfway through this book and suddenly decided you don't want to be in the Mafia. Too late, you can never get out alive. But assuming you have decided that The Life isn't the life for you because you're afraid of doing life, then I want to leave you with two things: a colorful mob nickname, let's hypothetically call you something like "Big Weenie"; and a quick tear-out chart that you can carry with you so you can act as your own Consigliere. Because the truth is, everyone needs good sound advice.

*Note:* The following things happen to ordinary people every day, so be sure to carry this helpful chart in your wallet.

✂ -------------------------------------------------

SITUATION: You loan a guy five large and he's two weeks behind on the interest. Now, let's complicate it, the guy is your son-in-law.

DON'T whack off his nuts, after all, you want some male heirs.

Do break his leg, because if non-family members see you do that, they'll be more likely to pay up on time.

SITUATION: You're at your favorite restaurant and the waiter brings you some veal. You're about to take a bite and you notice a hair in it.

DON'T go in the back and stick the chef's hand down the garbage disposal. After all, he needs that hand to cook with.

Do: This is where you cut off his nuts. He don't need them to cook with.

SITUATION: Your wife is telling her friends over coffee at Starbucks that you're having trouble with a limp sauseech.

DON'T show up at the place where they make porn films in South Jersey and ask for a part in a movie called *When Carla Does Camden.*

Do buy the missus a nice piece of jewelry. In exchange, she promises to walk around bowlegged for a week telling everyone you've been doing a job on her like when you were dating.

SITUATION: An overeager associate steals money from a joint protected by a rival family. The wiseguy whose turf your overeager associate has defiled asks for the money back plus the hand of your overeager associate. DON'T send him the money and the hand.

DO send him the money; send your associate out west to the protection of another family, and as a gesture of goodwill, send the guy a finger from your overeager associate.

SITUATION: The senator whose campaign you have contributed to for the past twelve years suddenly announces he is opening up an investigation of the business you work in. DON'T call him and angrily demand an explanation.

DO double your contribution to the senator. The entire reason he made that announcement was to get more money from you. These people are the real organized criminals.

SITUATION: In a loud voice, someone in a bar announces that Frank Jr. was not half the singer his old man was. DON'T carefully explain how Frank Jr. was actually a talented arranger who helped guide his father in the twilight of his career.

DO cut the guy's brake cables.

SITUATION: You're a young man with a promising future. Your father-in-law wants you to join The Life. Your father wants you to join his plumbing business. DON'T become a wiseguy.

Do become a plumber. Where do you think the Gottis made all their real money over the years? Wiseguys drive 1997 Lincolns, plumbers drive new Lincolns—every year.

## Lawyers and Consiglieri

A lawyer is different from a Consigliere. A Consigliere is a valued adviser, a man you would trust with your life, the one who speaks for you when it is time to reason with others. A lawyer is a whore. (Wait, that's an insult to whores.) At times, lawyers, like whores, are necessary. How do you know the difference between a good mob lawyer and a bad one? This should help.

Good mob lawyer: Delays, fights, and stalls the investigation until everyone is dead and it doesn't matter anymore. Like the lawyers for the tobacco industry.
Bad mob lawyer: Tells the Feds, "If my guy did what you said he did, he should be locked up."

Good mob lawyer: Tells the jury you are drooling because of a mental problem.
Bad mob lawyer: Tells the jury it's an act.

Good mob lawyer: Hides assets from prying eyes.
Bad mob lawyer: Takes your assets and opens a TCBY shop.

## My Son the M.D.: The Mob Doctor

You always hear about mob lawyers, but what about mob doctors? Is this a career that a young man or woman in medical school should consider? And if you would like to explore this new and exciting career option, do you want to be on the "healing end" of the mob medical profession or the "diagnosis end"?

Mob doctors on the "healing end" generally treat two types of medical problems for their mob patients: incredibly bad acne and multiple gunshot wounds to the body. With the gunshot wounds, unlike the acne, there is a chance of actually healing a mob patient.

Mob doctors on the "diagnosis" end are usually asked to use their knowledge of the human body to pinpoint exactly how far and in which orifice to jam the ice pick when trying to get a rival gang member to talk.

Here are five other common medical procedures a mob doctor is asked to perform:

An earectomy

A thumbectomy

A nonanesthesia lobotomy

Removing a baseball bat from the large colon

Prescribing penicillin after a date

## Middle Mob Management: Other Employment Opportunities

Every man has his destiny, as the great Vito Corleone once said. Or maybe it was Tony Robbins.* Some are

*The difference is that Don Corleone never got divorced.

destined to become Godfathers, others will become Consiglieri, still others will become corpses. But what about those of you who prefer to fill a supporting role? What about those of you who don't want the pressure and mortality rate of being upper management, but prefer instead to make a living in a middle-management position. The good news: There are plenty of middle-management Mafia careers available for people just like you. And you will note that all of these great career opportunities have two things in common:

1. They involve businesses that deal in cash.
2. They allow one to launder money. For the naive among you, laundering money doesn't mean leaving a C-note in the pocket of your Gap jeans when you throw them in the washer.

And what skills do you need if you want to work for the Mafia? The ideal job candidate has five basic skills (what your Mafia talent scouts call a "five-tool player"):

1. A willingness to lie to a loved one, your minister, or a police officer
2. A desire for easy money, tawdry sex, and great pasta
3. A lack of any remorse or guilt
4. No fear of burning in Hell
5. Ownership of a baseball bat

You may note that four of these five skills are also what it takes to succeed in the entertainment business; the one difference is that most people in Hollywood do not have their own baseball bats.

## The Five Best Mob Jobs

It's easy to figure out how to make money in the Mafia; it's impossible to figure out how to make money in an Internet startup company. Knowing that in advance, we begin . . .

### Loan-sharking

Loan sharks are guys who lend money for a short term at exorbitant interest rates, for example, the people at Wells Fargo Bank—although with loan sharks, it's easier to get approval for a business loan, plus there's a lot less paperwork. Pretty much all a loan shark wants to know is how much the borrower (aka "the fish") needs, how much he will pay back each week, and in the event the borrower is late, which thumb does he use the least.

In addition, a loan shark needs two things before going into business: a roll of fifty g's to put out on the street, and someplace to dispose of excess thumbs.

Now the novice may ask, Why do loan sharks tend to cut off the thumbs of delinquent borrowers? Because the thumb has fewer bones than an index finger and is easier to hack off,* and because deep

*See *The Pope of Greenwich Village.*

down, loan sharks have compassion. Thumbs are rarely used in sex.

## The Numbers

The numbers are also called the poor man's lottery. They are a way for a legitimate businessman to provide a necessary service to the neighborhood and a way for the average Joe to keep his winnings without paying off Uncle Sam. Look at those schmucks who won that $363 million Big Game Lottery. After they divided it up, paid taxes, hired a financial adviser, and cashed the check, they got about $2.63. And let's be honest, Uncle Santo Traficante did a hell of a lot more for poor folks than Uncle Sam. There are numbers writers and numbers runners. A *numbers writer* is the guy who keeps the records on "flash paper," a thin, tissuelike substance that can be destroyed with a drop of water. The *numbers runner* goes through the neighborhood collecting money and bringing the proceeds back to the writer. Oftentimes the numbers writer can branch out and become a loan shark

## Rules for Becoming a Successful Numbers Writer

Rule 1: Do not drool (see below).

Rule 2: Be good at math. (Einstein would have been a great numbers writer.)

Rule 3: Always carry a flash roll to impress the bettors and the cops. Carry it in a rolled up sock in your pants to impress the women.

Rule 4: Pay off in a timely manner.
Rule 5: Stay away from anyone who always plays
   the number 666.

*Important note:* If you have a tendency to drool, do not become a numbers writer. One ill-timed drop of spit can wipe out thousands of dollars' worth of flash paper betting slips making you, the writer, liable. So if you have a tendency to drool a lot, the next career is better suited for you.

## Enforcers

There are white-collar mob guys and blue-collar mob guys. Technically, all members of the Mafia are black collar, but my point is white-collar mob guys are the ones with a good head on their shoulders even though one day it may end up in some swamp on Staten Island. They run the numbers and the loan-sharking and the money end. Blue-collar mob guys are built like the U.S. Women's Olympic softball team—about 6 feet 2 inches and 250 pounds—and are named Jilly or Tiny or Luca or Fat Mo and their job is to enforce things. That's where drooling a lot can help. It can be very intimidating.

Enforcers can also be little pricks with big guns, but either way, somebody in the Mafia has to make sure that people play by the rules or there is chaos. If we had only sent in enforcers against Hitler in 1933 the whole war could have been avoided. And let's be honest, everyone uses enforcers who know how to intimidate someone with a baseball bat—look at the Yankees and Roger Clemens.

## Those "Lose Weight Quick" Schemes

This is probably the biggest moneymaking enterprise for the Mafia. You see the signs and posters everywhere: "Lose 25 pounds in 10 days. Call 555-1212 now. Ask us how." Totally mob controlled. The call comes into a mob storefront, the pigeon sends in $30, and then the mob "weight-loss expert" reveals the secret to losing weight.

### QUIT EATING SO FRIGGING MUCH!

This is better than the "address envelopes at home" scam and almost as good a money machine as Save the Children.

And amazingly, this weight-loss scheme actually works.

All you need to run this business is a Xerox machine, a staple gun to put up posters, a neighborhood with telephone poles, and a lot of chubby housewives.

EATS A LOT

HAS NOT EATEN SINCE 1979

## Congressman

Finally, the other all-time favorite profession for organized criminals is Congress. Remember, there is an old-world expression that describes all elected officials: *"Sono tutti una massa di ladri"*—They're all a bunch of crooks.

## The Exciting World of the Mob and Computers

Don Corleone once said that a lawyer with a briefcase could steal more money than a thousand men with guns could steal. And a mobster with a laptop and a DSL line can steal more than a thousand lawyers. What? You think any of that shit on eBay is real? It's one mob guy in a warehouse signing another million Joe DiMaggio autographed baseballs, another guy forging certificates of authenticity, and three guys in a truck shipping them out to all the fools who are paying $200 for a baseball worth $3.99.

And if you want to cripple the competition, you don't need to firebomb his business or break his legs. Just send one of his employees a funny e-mail with a virus attached. Or if you really want to bring his business to a halt, get his workers hooked on www.clublove or www.amihotornot. Within a week he'll have no money coming in, angry customers, and he'll agree to let you take over his operation for ten cents on the dollar.

Yes my friends, computers, that's where today's mobster is going. Did you know the mob won't even think of hiring you if you can't handle an Excel spreadsheet. And to give you an idea how sophisticated the mob has become, they are now whacking people with computers. Here's how it's done: Find where your victim works. Arrange to meet him in the office. Show up for your appointment. Hit him over the head with a laptop.* Drop the laptop, make sure you used that special tape so it leaves no fingerprints. Walk out briskly, don't look at anyone directly but don't hide your face either. Wear a hat so it gives eyewitnesses a chance to change their description of you after your associates have approached them.

Congratulations, you have now completed the chapter on making a living. Now it's time for an aptitude test to see which mob job you are best suited for. Match your physical, emotional, and intellectual description to the job applicant below and see what jobs (mob and non-mob) you qualify for.

## Job Match

1. You are 6 feet 3 inches, weigh 300 pounds, have a tattoo that says "born to die young," a thick mustache, and . . . you are a 23-year-old woman. You qualify for:
   a. Topless dancer in a mob-owned club
   b. Transvestite priest who hears confessions from rival mob members and sells them to the highest bidder

*Think outside the mob box. The laptop is the twenty-first-century equivalent of the baseball bat.

c. Telemarketer in "lose-weight quick" scam

d. Sexy voice on the end of a mob-owned 1-900 sex line

*Note:* The worst choice for you is "d," because all the women on the end of those sex lines are 6 feet 3 inches, 300 pounds with tattoos and mustaches, but they're 55 years old. You are too young.

2. You are named Sidney Hershberg. You are 5 feet 1 inch, weigh 122 pounds, and are a whiz with numbers. You qualify for:

a. Mob doctor (it would make your mother so proud)

b. Mob accountant (not as good as a doctor but you're still a professional)

c. Mob jockey (over your mother's dead body)

d. Gigolo (in your dreams)

3. You are cunning; intelligent; well-read in both Machiavelli and Sun-tzu, as well as Stephen Covey; plus you have no morals and are willing to lie and kill and cover up the murder. You are qualified for:

a. Godfather

b. L.A. police officer

c. Game-show host

d. Murder Inc.

e. HMO doctor

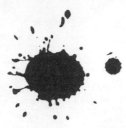

# 4

## Living the Life at Home

There's no place like home.

—Judy Garland as Dorothy in *The Wizard of Oz*

## The Mob Home

Once you are in the mob, you will always have a good living. Which means you will have money to buy your own place so you can live your life in The Life.

The key to finding the right mob home can be summed up in three words: location, location, location. The ideal mob home should be near a swamp and a funeral home. The swamp is for burying your enemies; the funeral home is for burying your friends. It should also be near a bakery, a topless club, and a pay phone.

*This is a typical mob house for a low-level soldier with a declared income of $13,000 a year.*

Of course it should also be near a well-respected, highly accredited school for the kids. Especially if you're selling drugs to them.

Riddle: When is a mob house not a mob home?
Answer: When it doesn't have lawn ornaments.

*The house on the top is worth $325,000; the one on the bottom is priceless.*

## The Typical Mob Family

Life in the mob is about more than just joining a family. It involves having a family. But to make sure you have the right type of family, you need to be aware that the typical mob family *must* include the following:

GRANDMOM: She is a widow; she is always ninety-eight years old; she dresses only in black, weighs either 73 or 245 pounds, and spends her day cooking (the 73-pound model), eating (the 245-pound model), and giving everyone in the neighborhood the evil eye. Goes by Grandma, Bubby, or anything but Mummsy (how many junior league mob grandmas do you know?).

Grandmom is always named: Concetta, Sylvia, Dolores, or Miriam.

DAD: He is the type of guy who brought a date to his wedding. He cheated on his honeymoon, he cheated while Mom was in labor, he's the type that tries to cheat with the nurse as he's getting an MRI ("Hey, two of us can fit under this"). Yet he claims that the most important thing to him is his family and the mother of his children. There have been spotty reports of a mob dad actually having all of his original hair, but these sightings, like those of Sasquatch, have never been confirmed. And speaking of Sasquatch, the mob dad marks his territory. At home, in the few minutes of the day when he is not threatening to slap his kids upside the head, he is taking a dump of toxic proportions. We are talking about an accumulated buildup of thirty years of garlic just exploding out of his colon. The swamps aren't the reason New Jersey smells like that.

Dad can be named either Tony or Hesh.

MOM: Every mob wife is expected to be a saint in public and a whore in the bedroom. There are two problems with this. First, somewhere along the way, signals get crossed and the average mob mom becomes a whore in public and a saint in the bedroom. The second problem is, whoever came up with this in the first place is an idiot. Guys, who wants a whore in the bedroom? They stare at the ceiling, they move less than the line at the DMV, and they can't even fake it. Or so I've been told.

But the mob mom is a good mom. She is strict—as in wait till your father gets home; she's a good cook—if you believe in quantity over quality; and most important, she's a credible alibi witness—"Honest, Herman could never have been there, he was with me all night."

Mom can be named: Sandy, Angie, Mindy, Mandy, or June.

THE OLDEST SON: He is told time and time again that he should study hard, do good in school, learn a profession, and stay out of the family business. At some point, generally when the parents realize he is seventeen and still in the fourth grade, the family reluctantly accepts the hand that fate has dealt them and they turn him over to an older uncle for instruction in the ways of the family.

It doesn't matter what he's named, he is always called Junior.

THE DAUGHTER: Smart as a whip with a mouth on her like a drunken sailor, she will invariably follow her mother's advice to hold out on boyfriends and retain her virginity—until she turns thirteen. At that point, she will begin a period of nonstop sexual frenzy that will last until the second she gets married. She is invariably close to grandmom, who will remind her as she marches down the aisle with that five-carat ring on her finger, that she will never ever ever have to give a blow job again.

She can be named: Heather, Brittany, Ashley, or anything that will enable her to try to pass as a WASP.

Remember, this book was written because the mob is on the endangered species list. The only way to save it in the short term is by recruiting and training people like you. But once we have you signed up and certified, we can begin our long-term plan, to swell the numbers of the herd by breeding our own. And that begins with . . .

## Dating and Courtship

Never forget that women are saints. They are the mothers of our children, they keep men in line, and they are God's angels on earth. So when dating, always treat a broad with respect. Remember, the woman stripping at a topless club is somebody's daughter. Or mother. Or grandmother. So here are ten rules to make sure you follow the proper dating etiquette.

RULE 1. *Show up on time and make sure she knows it.* That way, you establish a much-needed alibi if the rest of your family is out doing something you don't want to testify about. When you get to the door, announce in the loudest possible voice what time it is so everyone within earshot will remember what time you arrived. For example, you ring the doorbell, she answers, and you say "You are one classy broad for 8:07 at night."

RULE 2. *Always dress nice.* If it's a casual date, wear your blue jogging suit, if it's formal, wear black.

RULE 3. *Bring flowers.* Women love flowers. And if you live in a typical mob neighborhood, there are plenty of flowers available at the local funeral home when somebody meets an untimely demise. When Carlo Gambino died there were 110 cars filled with flowers in his procession. The more I think about it, in my next life, I'm going to sell Burpee seeds.

RULE 4. *Take her someplace nice.* Don't even think your date is going to want to spend the entire night at the Badda Bing Badda Boom topless club. No, women have class. Take her to dinner first.

RULE 5. *Always wear protection during sex.* It may be uncomfortable, it may not feel the same, but in this day and age, only an idiot has sex without wearing a bulletproof vest.

RULE 6. *Remember, women like it one way.* None of them digs a guy who goes down like a Russian submarine.

RULE 7. *Never date a girl who wears an underwire bra.* It could contain a real wire.

RULE 8. *If things are a bit slow in the romance department, frisk her before a date.* And there's nothing wrong with a full-body cavity search either. *Capisce?*

RULE 9. *When the time to do the honorable thing is ripe, ask her father for her hand in marriage.* It's old-fashioned plus you've already had all the good parts, so what harm is there in asking for her hand.

RULE 10. *Buy her a rock.* Enough said. Size and hardness does matter in only one thing—diamonds.

## Mafia Marriage

Weddings can be very simple or very complicated. For many of you, they are the last time you'll be dressed up and remembered fondly until your funeral, so here's a guide on the way to do it right.

THE PROPOSAL: This usually begins with the man looking deeply into his woman's eye or eyes and asking "You're having my what?" This is quickly followed by the second question, "How do you know it's mine?" After numerous assurances—all lies—that the mob guy was the mob girl's one and only, the wedding date is set.*

THE BEST MAN: This is the guy you would trust with your life. Because if you don't, right after you

---

*The mob girl should lay the groundwork for this later lie on the very first date with frequent references to a childhood horseback-riding accident.

kiss your bride, you have to kiss him on the mouth. Since you do trust him, you want to bestow an honor on him and let him know that wherever you go, he goes, right up until the time the two of you are sitting next to each other on death row.

THE BACHELOR PARTY: The best man has two jobs: (1) plan the bachelor party; (2) prescreen the X-rated video to make sure nobody's sister is in it. Or grandmother. Face it, you do not want to be watching Grandmom asking some poolboy if he likes it with teeth in or out.

Sometimes the best man will arrange a kidnapping. Not of the groom. Of some rich businessman who is held for ransom, which is how the wedding gets paid for.

THE MAID OF HONOR: The maid of honor is perhaps the busiest person at a mob wedding. She is the one who encourages everyone to dance. She is there to provide last-minute advice to the bride on how to pretend to still be a virgin (Hint #1: Leave the room dark and keep your pantyhose on). And she is there to take care of Sonny Corleone.*

THE SHOWER: We strongly recommend that both the bride and groom shower at least a week before the wedding.

PREHONEYMOON BIKINI WAXING: This is optional for the groom.

REGISTERING: Whenever you leave the state, you need to register with your parole officer.

*See scene with Lucy Mancini in *The Godfather.*

THE CEREMONY: Mafia wedding etiquette experts recommend a small ceremony, four hundred, maybe five hundred people. Three hundred of these will be siblings or first cousins. To seat and frisk that many, you will need a minimum of twelve ushers. It is of critical importance for the mob couple to hold the ceremony in a church, synagogue, or mosque. Not for religious purposes, but because police can't arrest anyone in a house of worship.

THE GOWN: The bride should wear white. The FDA has more things to worry about than truth in labeling. It is also important to remember that the mob tradition is slightly different when it comes to wearing "something old, something new, something borrowed, something blue." The mob tradition is "something old, something new, something stolen, something blue."

THE BAND: All you need is a good accordion player. However, there will be times when you'll need a full band. Call Tony at Musicians Local 1272 in Bayonne, he'll take care of you.

GIFTS FOR THE USHERS AND BRIDESMAIDS: You could give them each an engraved mug or a commemorative plate with the names of the happy couple and the date. You could do that—if you are some kind of freakin' civilian. You're in the mob! Give them something they can remember, like a tip on a horse at Aqueduct.

THE CAKE: Since the average mob guy spends $500 a week on cannolis, the baker should be happy to provide the cake free of charge.

THE HONEYMOON: Every couple should honeymoon somewhere completely foreign and exotic for two weeks. Like South Jersey. This way, if you're bored, you can always take a quick side trip to Atlantic City and try to double your wedding purse. Plus, if you're really bored, Atlantic City is known for its twenty-four-hour discount hookers.

PHOTOGRAPHER: There is no need to hire a photographer. If you are really in the mob, the Feds will have at least thirty people taking plenty of pictures. Two weeks after the ceremony, have your lawyer file a court order asking for copies. The federal marshals in Kansas are especially nice—they provide double prints. If you're not in the mob yet, leak to the *Globe* that Brad and Jennifer will be there. They'll take all the pictures you'll ever need.

### A Note on Mixed Marriages

Things have changed. Nowadays, you see more and more mixed marriages between a mob member and a civilian. In the old days, mixed marriages were an *infamata,* but times have changed. Especially given the fact that deep down, everyone is a frigging crook.

### Sex the Mob Way

Other than the rule about certain sexual acts being unmanly, the rule about having sex is pretty simple. Your partner should be alive and, at least 50 percent of the time, awake.

And if every act of sex was supposed to be for pro-creation, then half of us would look like tonsils.

Many of you may be wondering, after the hectic wedding and reception, what is the rule about sex on the wedding night? Sure, but make sure you drive right home afterwards to your new wife.

## Child Raising

Child raising is not to be confused with child rearing. Child raising happens in a mob home. Child rearing happens on a campout with funny scoutmaster Uncle Roy. There are three important rules to raising a child in a mob family:

RULE 1: Forget Dr. Spock. A misbehaving child should be handled like a juror—bribed, threatened, or shown that a belt is not just for holding up pants.

RULE 2: You are a role model for your kids. If they see you show weakness, if they see you forgive a guy who's behind on his payments because of some sob story, then they're likely to show weakness when they're collecting lunch money from the other kids. Never forget that the little ones imitate everything you do.

RULE 3: Sibling rivalry is natural, dropping a dime on someone is not. Teach them that *omertà* is not just for those who are indicted.

So, now it is time to see if you can handle the first step toward having your own family . . .

# Do You Have What It Takes to Be a Mob Lover?

1. During sex you usually
   a. Scream out your partner's name
   b. Plead the Fifth Amendment
   c. Scream out your own name

2. Sex is best
   a. With the lights on
   b. With the lights off
   c. With the dashboard light on

3. If your partner pulls a Nelson Rockefeller and dies while in the saddle, your immediate reaction is to
   a. Scream and roll off
   b. Call 911
   c. Finish

4. Your lover suggests something innovative, like handcuffs. Your reaction is to
   a. Try it, you might like it
   b. Announce politely that handcuffs are not your thing
   c. Wonder how you can use the TV remote during sex if you're handcuffed

5. Your partners are usually
   a. Blond
   b. Brunette
   c. Inflatable

6. After sex you
   a. Think about how long until you can make love again
   b. Hang up on the phone sex operator
   c. Thank the priest

Give yourself 3 points for every time you answered "a," 1 point for every "b," if you answered "c" just kill yourself because you are a sick loser.

• • • • • • • • • • • • • • • • • • • • • • • • • • • • • • • • • • •

SCORING

12–18 points: Last of the red-hot mob lovers.

10–11: A good mob lover.

7–9: You're no Johnny Stompanato; if you're planning to stay in the mob, you might want to carry a rolled up sock in the pocket.

4–6: If you make love like this, you shouldn't be in the mob, you should be in a cemetery.

0–3: Forget the mob, just go to a Star Trek convention.

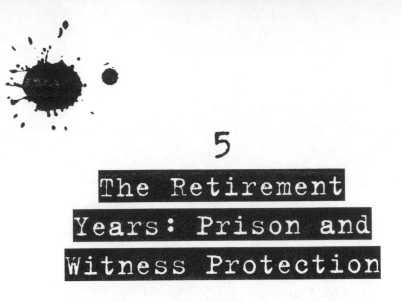

# 5

# The Retirement Years: Prison and Witness Protection

You want to be the mommy or the daddy?

—Graffiti on cellblock wall of
Folsom State Prison

**The first** thing to do is to not think of prison as a bad thing; think of it as part of every mobster's life. Because despite all this good advice, there are times and circumstances where you make a mistake. There are two types of mistakes you make in The Life—fatal and nonfatal. Fatal mistakes involve eating with the wrong guy in the wrong restaurant and ending up kissing cement. Nonfatal mistakes are less serious and lead to spending time in jail trying not to be kissed by some *finocchio* named Rodney. This chapter deals with how to survive and make good use of your time in the penitentiary.

First of all, no one in the mob actually likes to use the word *prison*. Try these euphemisms instead . . .

## Other Phrases That Mean Prison
The golden years
A vacation courtesy of the federal government
A time-share at Leavenworth
Government-subsidized three square meals a day
A sabbatical

## Your First Day in the Slammer

Think of jail as like being back in high school. The only difference is that in high school, if they think you're a pussy, you don't get a prom date; in prison, if they think you're a pussy, you are the prom date.

But the good news: The fact you are a made guy will help as long as you make it known. My suggestion is this: As you are being escorted to your cell, say in a loud voice, "Anyone comes near me and I turn their mother into spaghetti bolognese." Second, and this is going to be uncomfortable but *it must be done:* Carry your flash roll where the sun don't shine. This accomplishes two things: First, it enables you to bribe the guard to make sure you have a cell by yourself. And second, in the event you drop the soap in the shower, your roll of hundreds is a good first defense.

## Prison Jobs

There are only two acceptable jobs to have in prison. One is a job as the warden's secretary. Why, you may ask, does a Tough Guy want a job usually held by broads? Because that's where the telephones are and that's how you can continue to run and keep in touch with your organization. Here's an example of how it's done.

YOU IN PRISON: It's me.
YOUR SECOND IN COMMAND: How youse doing?
YOU IN PRISON: Good. I hear the guy from the other place better watch out or he could catch a cold.
YOUR SECOND IN COMMAND: You want me to see him to see if he's sneezing?
YOU IN PRISON: Yes.
YOUR SECOND IN COMMAND: Got it.

Now that you're in the life, it's absolutely clear what this conversation is about. Guy #1 is telling Guy #2 to cut off the hand of one of Frankie the Cat's pimps to keep him from hassling your working girls at the truck stops, and if that doesn't work, to take Frankie the Cat to meet that big Godfather in the sky.

The only other acceptable job in prison is on death row, because it's fun.

## Five Ways to Pass the Time in Jail

Exercise
Read
Recruit new family members
Make personalized license plates for your loved
   ones

Start corresponding with one of those fat desperate trailer park chicks who always fall in love with guys doing time. You can get names and addresses in *Prison Life Magazine.*

Most of all, be a man, accept your sentence and do the time with pride.

But what about those of you who don't want a taxpayer-subsidized vacation. That brings us to . . .

## Witness Protection

This is also a taxpayer-subsidized vacation, albeit one on the outside rather than on the inside. To get into the witness protection program, you must be willing to sell out your friends, your family, your business associates, and everything you've stood for. On the other hand, playing golf in Hawaii is a lot better than fifteen years trying to keep from getting a nonconsensual colonoscopy. Let's see: golf course versus involuntary anal intercourse. Tough choice.

If you chose witness protection, you need to know how to cut a good deal. Sammy the Bull cut a bad deal. Who in their right mind wants to live in Arizona . . . and work construction. Don't believe that crap that he had his own company. Here's a guy who used to put people in cement and he ends up pouring cement for the highway crew? In 125-degree heat? Wearing a black jumpsuit? No wonder he turned back to The Life.

Now take that Elián Gonzalez kid, the one from Cuba; he cut a deal. An eleven-hundred-acre estate in Maryland, plus a new yellow slide, plus the Toys "R" Us platinum card.

No, when you cut the deal, you want a good location like Vegas or Paris or East Orange, New Jersey, and you want a cash-generating job where you don't have to work like a dog. Ask to become a mortgage broker, which is really just a loan shark with a junior college degree and a business card. Plus, for your new look, demand a good plastic surgeon. Not one of those army doctors who are always secretly working on Hillary Clinton. No, you want the cutters they bring in when they've got a massive facial reconstruction to do, like with land mine victims or Tori Spelling.

But how can you tell if you should choose prison or witness protection? Because you have to be able to handle either or you shouldn't be in the mob. As always, we turn now to our test.

## Prison or Witness Protection: What Kind of Mob Retirement Is for You?

It's a very simple test. Put down this book and go out to the grocery store. Buy three jalapeños, three garlic cloves, some bad clams, and a container of Metamucil. Mix in the blender. Drink it quickly. Spend the next two days in the bathroom. If you are able to stand up straight after your ass has taken a pounding like that, you can handle prison. If not, witness protection is for you.

# 6

## Minestrone
## for the Mob Soul

### Five Stories to Open the Heart
### and Rekindle the Mob Spirit*

Mmm mmm good,
Mmm mmm good
That's what Campbell's soups are
Mmm mmmm good
—**Those annoying Campbell's Soup twins**

Mmmmmmmmmmmm . . .
—**Sound made by a gagged mob informant**
**as he sinks into the East River**

The names of these people have been changed to protect the guilty. Any resemblance to fictional characters seen on TV who get nominated a lot but don't win as many Emmys as "West Wing" is purely coincidental, the same way it was coincidental that Jack Ruby and Lee Harvey Oswald knew each other before November 1963.

*Or, as we would say in the mob, five stories to cut out your heart and rekindle a suspicious fire.

## On Growing Up Mobster

*People ask me all the time what's it like to be the son of Tony Alto. First of all, it means you never get picked last in gym class. Second, it means you never even have to take gym class. What phys. ed. teacher wants to see me with a baseball bat? Third and most important, I not only have every video game a kid could ever want, but for two months I was the Sony PlayStation 2 dealer in my school.*

*So overall I'd say having a dad like my dad is pretty cool. We are pretty close. We do all kinds of neat things like play marbles, go to ball games, and play the ponies. Real father-son stuff. Stuff I want to do with my son. Okay, I admit it, there's never going to be a Junior Alto Junior. I don't like girls. I don't want to be a mob guy. I want to sing and dance. I don't want to hit people, I want a hit on* Broadway. *I'm writing a musical about life in the mob. I'm still working on the title. How does this sound:* A Funny Thing Happened on the Way to an Honest Living; *or the* Lying Kings; *or* There's No Business like Mob Business?

*Mom knows. And so does Father Frank. In fact, Father Frank is the one who . . . never mind.*

*—Junior Alto*

## On Second Marriages

*I'm not the first Mrs. Alto. No, the first Mrs. Alto was the sainted Mary Teresa. I'm just the JB from Brooklyn. The homewrecker. The Judith Nathan of the mob.*

*What can I say, God gave me a gift and I used it to land the man of my dreams. Is it my fault there was a nailbomb on his front porch that made the sainted first Mrs. Alto look like a two-hundred-pound Swiss cheese? That's right, Tony whacked his own wife. And that's why I am who I am today, the mob queen of New Jersey.*

*And you better believe it, the other women in The Life have to give me respect. They go to lunch when I want to go to lunch, they eat lunch where I want to eat lunch, and when we go to see the Chippendales, I get first dance.*

*Sure, our marriage has had its ups and downs. Like the fact we live in goddamned Hoboken. Like the fact that nobody really cares that I'm the mob queen of New Jersey. Like the fact that electrolysis doesn't seem to work anymore. Like the fact that I think Tony may have cheated on me. Don't say I'm crazy. Women have a sixth sense about these things. For example, I think it's not a good thing that twice in the last year Tony burned all our linen and started using Kwell. I guess you can catch them from wearing someone else's hat. But anyway, if Kathie Lee can stand by her man and if Anne Heche can stand by her woman and man, then Carmella Rothberg Alto is going to stand by her man because half of the money he makes is mine.*

*—Carmella Alto*

## On Going Away to College

*My name is Brook Alto, I am eighteen years old, I am a freshman at Swarthmore College, and I hate my dad. Do you know what it's like living with a failed cretin? I have six words that sum it all up: "Take our daughters to work day." Brittany went with her dad to his Wall Street investment house and worked with him on the Cisco Arrowpoint buyout. Heather went with her mom to the hospital where she's a pediatrician and helped her deliver a baby. Suzy went with her dad to his restaurant and made an ice sculpture. And what did Brook Alto do? I watched my dad stab a guy with an ice pick because he made fun of Tina Sinatra. Who the hell even knew there was a Tina Sinatra? I thought I knew all the lesser Sinatras and I had no idea who she was. She must not have posed nude.*

*So this is my plan. I'm staying one semester at Swarthmore, getting a nose job at government expense, changing my name to something really WASPy like Brooke Astor, and transferring to Stanford.*

*—Brook Alto*

## On Having Kids

*Your life changes the minute you become a father. One minute it's just you and the missus going out to dinner, living the good life, the next thing you know, you've got kids to worry about. It changes you. You start to think of your own mortality a lot more. I know I went out and doubled my life insurance. I hired two body-guards.*

*I even thought about leaving The Life, becoming a regular civilian, working nine to five, coming home to dinner every night, sitting at that table with the family. Then I started to picture what life is like for Joe Civilian, eating that cold goddamned meatloaf three nights a week, listening to the kids screaming about some toy we can't afford, watching a big-ass wife instead of a big-screen TV. I'd end up shooting myself instead of shooting other people. That's why I'm telling you, kids are wonderful as long as you don't have to spend any real time around them.*

*—Tony Alto*

## On Growing Old

*I have something important to say to all of you about what it's like to have a son who is in the mob. This is probably the most important thing you'll ever hear in your life, and it's certainly worth the price of this book. The secret to . . .*

(*Editor's Note:* In the middle of writing this, Livia Alto was found slumped over her desk with a meat cleaver in her head. The New Jersey state coroner ruled it a suicide.)

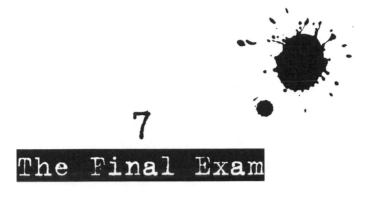

# 7

## The Final Exam

### Testing Your Mob IQ
### (Indictment Quotient)

**Attorneys** have to pass the bar exam before they can practice law; doctors have to be licensed by the state before they can practice medicine; undertakers have to be certified before they do those vile things to your dead body.* And you have to pass this test to see if you have what it takes to become a certified mob member. However, unlike the bar exam, you don't have three chances to pass. You've come this far, and you've learned a lot. If you've learned enough, you can join The Life. If you fall short, well, let's just say that you might want to think about term life insurance.

*And don't kid yourself. What they do late at night when no one is looking is beyond imagination. It's in the dictionary—necrophilia. Look it up. And they think being in the mob is sick.

## The Mob IQ Test

1. Fredo is to Michael like
   a. Cain was to Abel
   b. George W. Bush is to Jeb
   c. Tito Jackson is to Michael Jackson

2. A Brinks truck leaves the Bronx at 3 a.m. carrying $500,000 in cash. It is traveling at 45 mph to a destination in Queens 15 miles away. How long will it take to get there?
   a. Twenty minutes
   b. Thirty minutes
   c. Like the boys are going to ever let it arrive

3. Mob guys don't like to eat
   a. Matzoh ball soup
   b. A heavy veal dish with white wine
   c. South of the border . . .
   d. All of the above

4. When you see the underboss kiss the ring of his capo, it means
   a. He is pledging his loyalty forevermore
   b. He is setting him up to get hit later that night
   c. It means they're both lonely and yearning for the love that dares not speak its name
   d. Any of the above

5. There is one thing in this world that men in The Life cannot understand:
   a. Size really does matter
   b. The ways of a woman
   c. What Angelina Jolie is doing with Billy Bob Thornton

6. The lady in red
   a. Is the woman who set up John Dillinger
   b. $50
   c. J. Edgar Hoover in drag

7. Murder Inc. is
   a. An enforcement arm for La Cosa Nostra started by Lucky Luciano and Albert Anastasia that is responsible for between seven hundred and a thousand murders
   b. The nickname for the wardens of the Texas prison system
   c. What unarmed innocent African Americans call the NYPD

8. "Hard time" is what a guy in the life calls
   a. Serving time in a federal prison
   b. Being married to a Jewish American Princess
   c. Taking too many Viagra, not that a guy in The Life would ever need it

9. Maier Suchowljansky is
   a. The real name of Meyer Lansky
   b. The real name of Eminem
   c. Worth seven hundred points in Scrabble

10. The longest, bloodiest conflict in American history was
    a. The Five Families War of 1946
    b. Rudy Giuliani versus Donna Hanover
    c. Jeffrey Katzenberg versus Michael Eisner

● ● ● ● ● ● ● ● ● ● ● ● ● ● ● ● ● ● ● ● ● ● ● ● ● ● ● ● ● ● ● ●

Correct answers: 1-b or c, 2-c, 3-d, 4-d, 5-c, 6-b, 7-c, 8-b, 9-a or c, 10-b

SCORING:

Passing is 20 percent, about the same as George W. Bush's blood alcohol back in 1976.

If you got 9–10 correct, congratulations, you're a certified mob genius.

If you got 7–8 correct, you can be a good underboss.

If you got 5–6 correct, stick with the strong-arm stuff.

If you got 3–4 correct, stay away from the money end.

If you got 0–2 correct, for two large I'll fix it so it looks like a perfect ten.

# 8

## Top Secret
## Initiation Ceremony

**Congratulations!** If you are reading this chapter, it means you have passed the test and are now ready to join the mob.* Raise your right hand (the one missing the thumb) and repeat after me:

I (state full mob nickname) having read this book and passed the mob certification test, and being of sound mind and body, accept my entry into a new life in The Life. And with the training I have received, I acknowledge that if things don't work out, I can always run for Congress.

That's it. You're in. You are officially mob member #6.

*To those who did not pass the Chapter 7 test, Simon & Schuster will notify your next of kin.

# 9

## The Code of Conduct

### The Ten Commandments of Mob Living

Doctors have their Hippocratic Oath, the English have their Magna Carta, the Jews almost had the vice president of the United States and still have the Torah. And as newly certified wiseguys you also have a code, the Ten Commandments of being a mob guy. Please learn these. For if you follow this code of conduct, trust me, you will live a hundred years—give or take seventy-five.

*1. Thou shalt honor thy godfather.*
Let me explain. If you decide to work for the Mafia, you have to respect the fact that all organized crime families have just one guy in charge. Look at Microsoft and Bill Gates. Corporations have a CEO; the Mafia has its own version of a CEO. He's called the Godfather.

Whenever you have two guys in charge, it never works. This is why Ben and Jerry never had their own crime family. Although their Chunky Monkey ice cream has put more people in the grave than the Mafia. So remember, one guy in charge running the entire show—for example, Dick Cheney.

*2. There's money in trash.*
He who steals my trash steals gold. I think Jerry Lewis said that. Did you know his real last name was Levitch? And Dean Martin's real last name was Crocetti. Go figure, Dino Crocetti and Joseph Levitch. Anyway, there's money in trash. People hate having trash around and they will pay a ton of money to have it taken away. And trash can be recycled. Look at Hollywood.

And why is trash the equivalent of gold? Here's how it works. The Mafia buys (or in this case, leases) a local politician who passes a law making it mandatory that people recycle. Then the mob's "buyers" corner the market on those stupid different color trashcans, which are sold at a huge profit to homeowners. Next, all those limousine liberals spend hours sorting trash *for the mob*, which gets picked up in overweight trucks driven over highways paved with cheap mob cement. As a result, the highway gets potholes, bids are taken, and, lo and behold, the "leased" politicians award the contract to the high bidder because it is a minority-owned firm. Of course, this is not a real minority-owned firm; this is a subsidiary of the local mob with a minority partner as a "front man." So the local government is paying a mob construction company to fix the highways that the mob trucks ruined in the first place. It gets even better. Next the mob guys dump half the trash in one big pile in the goddamn swamp on top of some bodies, usually legitimate construction company owners who made the mistake of bidding on the aforementioned contract. The trash is dumped without bothering to separate it because who the hell is driving fifty miles in the Jersey swamps to see if anybody split paper from plastic, then the Mafia mixes the other half of the trash in the cement used to fix the highways and everyone is happy because Susie and Thad Average Citizen have no trash piled up on their front lawn, the taxpayers have new roads and the average mob guy and the leased politicians have pocketed about two hundred large a year to spend in area businesses, thus improving the local economy. It's a wonderful country.

So during your initial interview with the Mafia, let it slip in that you are interested in learning the waste management business.

*3. If, during a turf war, a guy you don't particularly like wants you to go to a restaurant you've never been to before, and then he asks you to sit with your back to the door, and then he excuses himself to go to the john, make like Phillip Michael Thomas and just disappear.\**

*Phillip Michael Thomas disappeared after a cast party of "Miami Vice" and has never been seen again.

That scene where Michael Corleone whacks the New York City police captain isn't some made-up piece of Hollywood crap. That happens in real life all the time. I saw this on the Internet—in May last year, a Jehovah's Witness got whacked in a Subway sandwich shop in Paramus for trying to steal some other guy's turf. And nobody is more jealous at protecting turf than the goddamned Girl Scouts. Just try to sell Thin Mints on the wrong side of the street and see what happens. You get your leg broken. So, to play it safe, let's review each part of commandment #3:

IF, DURING A TURF WAR (Probably the worst turf of the last fifty years occurred in Agoura Hills, California, in 1998 when two bagel shops opened right next to each other)

A GUY YOU DON'T PARTICULARLY LIKE (There are two types of people in the world: family and people trying to whack you. Unless they're blood, don't trust them.)

WANTS YOU TO GO TO A RESTAURANT YOU'VE NEVER BEEN TO BEFORE (Why would you go to a restaurant you've never been to before? First of all, why go somewhere where the owner doesn't know you? Second, they could poison you. Third, only go to places where you know in advance you're going to get a good meal, because you never know when it's going to be your last meal.)

AND THEN HE ASKS YOU TO SIT WITH YOUR BACK TO THE DOOR (Here is an updated version of a classic song: You don't tug on Janet Reno's dress, you don't spit on

Vincent the Chin, you don't ride bareback with a crack-addicted hooker, and you don't go to some frigging restaurant and sit with your back to the door so some eighteen-year-old trying to make his bones blows out your brains in a plate full of mussels.)

AND THEN HE EXCUSES HIMSELF TO GO TO THE JOHN, MAKE LIKE PHILLIP MICHAEL THOMAS AND DISAPPEAR. (No grown man ever has to go to the john in the middle of dinner and if a woman has to do it she's bulimic. Either way, get out of there.)

*4. If a guy you know won't take off his shirt at the Jersey Shore, it means he's got tits or he's wearing a wire. Either way, you want to see.*

True story: Three years ago a guy I know from the neighborhood was at a Labor Day picnic with Local 269 at Asbury Park. He told me later that while he was there, a guy named "Skinny Paulie" approached him. Remember, whenever a guy is named Teeny or Skinny, it means he's got a stomach on him the size of Nutley, New Jersey. My buddy and Skinny Paulie go down to the water to talk and my buddy notices two things: (1) it's ninety-five degrees, and (2) Paulie is wearing a T-shirt.

The T-shirt was very classy, something like "If Frank were alive, he'd kick Springsteen's skinny little Dutch ass." So my buddy gets suspicious. They're looking out at the ocean, they're talking and my buddy yells, "Look, there's a whale." Just as Skinny

Paulie looks, my buddy gets behind him and grabs him in a hug to see if he's wearing a wire. No wire. But my buddy said it was the best goddamned feel in his life.

*5. Real men don't mangia la pesca.*
How can I best explain this? It seems that all the young women today want the same thing. They all want guys to . . . how can I say this delicately . . . head south for the Australian bush. Which I guess is why they call Australia "down under."

*6. Insulate yourself from illegal enterprises.*
This is a reminder that every mob boss needs a Consigliere. What you tell your Consigliere is privileged information. It's like the things you tell your secretary while the two of you are on a business trip. We all know the rule: Anything that happens more than a hundred miles from town can't be held against you. A Consigliere won't testify against his boss just as a man can't testify against his wife. If you order somebody whacked, the Consigliere gets it done and you're protected. It's all part of the American system of justice.

*7. Let the Jews handle your books.*
Let's be honest, those people are a whiz with numbers. Meyer Lansky you can trust. Those *gonifs* at the big-eight accounting firms, fuhgeddaboutit.
*Point to remember:* There are always two sets of

books. The books you show the Feds and the books that show where the money really is. That's why when the Feds went to nail Capone, they went after the accountant. Even the people at the Academy Awards have two sets of books, one real, one rigged. That's how Marisa Tomei ended up with an Oscar.

*8. Own a strip club, don't visit one.*
About every five weeks, you hear about some poor schmuck who lost his house, his credit cards, and his life savings because he spent $2,000 a week at strip clubs. And when they show this poor guy on TV, he always says the same thing: "I thought the stripper really liked me." Oh yeah, they all have hearts of gold.

Look, you can go through life as a fish or a shark. Fish are thirty-five-year-old bald accountants named Melvin who blow their paycheck on a twenty-five-year-old named Summer who slides down a firepole and shoves silicone in their face. Sharks are the ones who hired Summer in the first place, bought her the implants, took them for a test drive, and charge guys named Melvin a $20 cover and $10 for a watered-down gin and tonic. You decide: shark or fish? Tough call.

## Bonus Quiz to See if You're a Shark or a Fish

1. You buy a new Lincoln Continental. When you get it home, you realize that the salesman has left his brand-new $10,000 Rolex in the backseat. You

   a. Keep it

   b. Return it because you hope that the dealer will then be extra nice to you when you bring it in for service

   c. Show up at the salesman's house, find out how some polyester car-pimp making thirty large a year can afford a Rolex and make him cut you in for whatever action he has going on the side

2. You find out that while your wife was on a business trip, she contemplated having an affair with her boss. You . . .

   a. Kill him, divorce her

   b. Begin joint couples therapy to find out what issues she has with you that are troubling her

   c. Forget about it and use it as an excuse to go to Vegas with blond triplets

3. Your doctor tells you that you have six months to live. You immediately

   a. Kill the doctor

105

  b. Begin calling all the people you've wronged
     to ask forgiveness
  c. Forget about it and use it as an excuse to go
     to Vegas with blond triplets

4. A major Hollywood studio comes to you with a
   $500,000 proposal to turn your life story into a
   movie about the mob. Your response is to
   a. Kill the movie producer
   b. Wrestle with violating the sacred code of
      *omertà* and, ultimately, turn down the
      money but tell the movie producer enough
      information so he can make the movie with-
      out you
   c. Turn down the movie, take the money, leave
      the cannolis

5. Dominos shows up at your house forty-five
   minutes late with a sausage pizza. You had or-
   dered pepperoni. You
   a. Kill the delivery boy
   b. Gently remind him about the thirty-minute
      delivery policy and only give him a 14 per-
      cent tip
   c. Make the delivery boy star in your next porn
      movie because every porn movie has a pizza
      delivery boy

• • • • • • • • • • • • • • • • • • • • • • • • • • • • • • • • •

Give yourself 2 points for each "a" answer, 3 points for each "c" answer, and minus 200 for each "b" answer.

SCORING

12–15 points: You are a shark. You are at the top of the mob food chain.

8–11 points: You are neither shark nor fish, more like a dolphin. Sharks leave you alone but you really don't get to intimidate people.

5–7: You are a big fish. You've got a chance to survive in the open as long as there is a reef to protect you.

Under 4: You are such a miserable pathetic fish, send me $200 a week or I'll break your fins.

## 9. Be proud of your lifestyle.

Behind every great fortune is a crime. I'm not sure who said that, it was either Balzac or Regis. Either way, you need to accept the fact that some people will look down on the fact that you are in the Mafia. And, I will be honest with you, there are some drawbacks.

For one thing, it is very tough to get life insurance. For another thing, prison is not the place to be if you have attractive buttocks. That's about it, the only two drawbacks. So when those people look down on you, remember, you are in one of the world's oldest and most honored organizations. And you need to tell your critics that. Right before you kneecap them.

*Point to remember:* One thing that will be especially upsetting to the average civilian is the fact that guns are an integral part of The Life. The average guy in the Mafia has a sawed-off shotgun, an Uzi, and thirty-five handguns that are impossible to trace. And even he thinks the people in the NRA are frigging wackos.

### 10. Buy low, sell high.

You'd be amazed how many people get this confused. It's like feed a fever, starve a cold. Or is it starve a fever, feed a cold? See, it's confusing. And if you get this one backward and buy high and sell low, you are going to have some big financial problems. What kind of business can exist when it loses money year after year after year? Okay, other than Amazon.com.

# A Final Thought

The **main** thrust of this book has been that the Mafia is good for you and you can be good for the Mafia. And I bet JFK would appreciate the rip-off of his 1961 Inaugural Address to promote the very organization that ended up killing him. But let us not forget that you are about to enter a noble calling, for the Mafia is good for America. Think of this as your creed. As you read this, feel free to hum "America the Beautiful" . . . or "My Way."

## Why the Mafia Is Good for America

- The Mafia is good for America because, unlike the Republican Party, it is open to minorities.
- The Mafia is good for America because the mob got an Oscar nomination for Oliver Stone. What happened is they elected John F. Kennedy in 1960, he got us into Vietnam, Oliver Stone wrote a movie about it, got nominated for an Oscar, and then he paid JFK back by making a movie about his assassination. At least that's what the Warren Commission wants you to believe.
- The Mafia is good for America because without the mob Bing Crosby would have been more famous than Frank Sinatra, and without Frank we wouldn't have all that great music plus none of us would know you can actually eat scrambled eggs off the chest of a topless hooker.
- The Mafia is good for America because without them no one would have ever used the words *Big Pussy* on TV except Joan Rivers's gynecologist.
- The Mafia is good for America because without the Mafia we would not have Las Vegas, without Las Vegas we would not have Siegfried and Roy, and without Siegfried and Roy we would not have role models for same-sex marriages.

As always, the number five is key.

JON MACKS, author of *Heaven Talks Back* and *From Soup to Nuts,* is a writer for "The Tonight Show with Jay Leno." He has also written for the Academy Awards with Billy Crystal, the Emmy Awards, the American Comedy Awards, "Comic Relief" with Robin Williams, Billy Crystal, and Whoopi Goldberg, and "Hollywood Squares." He lives in Los Angeles with his wife and three children.